Living Between the Scans

That Time I Beat Pancreatic Cancer

David H. Robb

© 2015 David H. Robb

All Rights Reserved.

No part of this publication may be reproduced, stored in a retrieval system, or transmitted, in any form or by any means, electronic, mechanical, photocopying, recording, or otherwise, without the written permission of the author.

First published by Dog Ear Publishing
4011 Vincennes Rd
Indianapolis, IN 46268
www.dogearpublishing.net

dog ear
PUBLISHING

ISBN: 978-1-4575-4188-9

This book is printed on acid-free paper.

Printed in the United States of America

Contents

So Sorry 1

Decision Time 5

1st Chemo 6

Towards Our New Routine 7

Moving Along 8

Second Cycle 9

Off To Texas 10

Back From Houston – Now What? 12

Keeping An Open Mind 13

Time For Some Surgery 14

Dave In Recovery 16

New Chemo Is In – Feels Different 17

Captain Cold & His Gang 19

FOLFIRINOX Is A Frothy Can Of Whoop-Ass 21

You Can't Un-ring The Cancer Bell 24

Waiting For My Chemo..27

Milestones 29

Knocking The Tumors On Their Heels 33

Funny Story 35

Summertime, Swimming, Dishwashers, & More Chemo 37

You Meet A Lot Of People Along The Way 40

Back To School, Back To Houston 42

Here Comes The Radiation 45

They Gave Me Tattoos 49

Hair, Photons, & An Amazing Ride 52

Ringing The Raydonkulous Bell 56

Cancer – Year Two 59

It's Whipple Time! 61

Waiting..62

Whip The Cancer With A Whipple...66

Footprints In The Sand 67

The Cancer Is Gone...78

Slow Spring, Slow Healing 80

I'm Talking About Tomorrow 84

Jumping Into The Pool 86

Scans, Yoga, & Season's Greetings 89

The Perpetual Present..93

Living Between The Scans 95

So Sorry

I have to begin this book by saying that I'm sorry. I'm not sure that I've "beaten" my Stage IV pancreatic cancer. Only time will tell. As one of the doctors involved in my diagnosis said: "in the long-run, almost nobody survives this disease." Um, thanks for that, doctor. Anyway, if you bought this book based on the title and hoping that I have any special approach to "the cure," I am sorry, but I do not.

Early in my journey, as word spread of my illness, an old friend sent me a note of encouragement. She said she hoped that one day I could look back on this whole episode as "that time I beat cancer." At the time, it sounded like a naïve sentiment, but there was something about the hopefulness and the projection into the future of that statement that stuck with me. And here we are, more than two and a half years later – as of this writing – living in to what was then a hopeless, and possibly non-existent, future.

I'm sorry for another reason, too: if you are reading this book, it's probably because you or someone you love has pancreatic cancer. It's often hard to find the right words when it comes to cancer. As another one of the doctors put it: "it's a shitty break." To which my wife replied: "well...that's one way to say it."

That was back at the beginning, let's start there.

In December 2012, I fell ill. I was nauseas, had a decreased appetite, and was increasingly fatigued. I was also turning yellow. The last things to change color were my eyeballs, they turned yellow, too. There were some other digestive symptoms that were kind of gross. Cancer is pretty gross.

At 44, I had never been seriously ill, never broken or cut anything, never stayed in a hospital. Oh, and I used to be irrationally afraid of needles. I've passed out at the dentist before. Even came close once at the eye doctor – and there wasn't even a needle!

I was married with two young children and was about to learn that I had Stage IV pancreatic cancer.

As quickly as we got to the bottom of the diagnosis, we jumped into treatment. We started a Caringbridge.org page almost immediately. Having seen how helpful Caringbridge was for friends and family in the past, we wanted to use it to get the word out and start communicating with people.

As we've moved forward, I've maintained a journal there. The journal has kept friends and family informed but, equally important, I found it therapeutic to write about our family's cancer journey. It has turned into a sort of cancer blog.

Now, more than two years into our battle, I've decided to put this book together. Well, to be honest, I've mostly just taken the blog, tacked on a beginning and an ending, and fixed a few typos in between.

My purpose with this book is to take another step in my healing and, hopefully, to help others who may be dealing with this terrible disease. I want to offer a hopeful voice in the writings about pancreatic cancer. Too often, the outcome occurs too fast and the pain and discomfort is so great, that most first-hand accounts are very discouraging.

This book is also for my sons, so that they will have something to refer back to, regardless of how my story ultimately ends.

Please bear with me, I do not have any scientific or medical training. I'm not going to try and make sure I've got all of the medical terms and concepts correct, there are other places to look for that.

Please also remember that some of these posts were written in the middle of the night as I sat bleary-eyed in front of the computer, unable to sleep due to the steroids. Some of the posts were written under the influence of opioid pain medicine. Nonetheless, this is the story of my journey so far and how I have found a life between the scans. Subjective as it may be.

If you're in the cancer club, one of the first things they probably did was foist a rash of brochures on you. Or, worse still, point you toward some websites. I remember a three-ring binder with a particularly pretty cover. It was an Ansel Adams-style woodland photograph, but in a verdant color scheme. It sat on a shelf for about a year until I asked my wife if she had ever opened it. She said no, I dumped the contents in the trash, and we re-purposed the pretty green binder.

Perhaps the most absurd pamphlet we received was titled: "Sex and the Man with Cancer." Seriously? You just told me the average survival time for this is 6 months and you're handing me this pamphlet?

Anyway, let's get started. The first post was from my wife, Sabrina. I was too down-and-out at the time to write much of anything. She was also the one to post updates following my surgeries and I've Included those, too.

Christmas 2012, just before our world turned upside-down

Decision Time

Written Jan 8, 2013 7:31pm by Sabrina Robb

Yesterday we met with the surgeon and today with the oncologist. At this time, Dave is not a good candidate for surgery. He is in the process of deciding between the different treatment cocktails and expects to begin treatment this week. Please keep him in your prayers and send him your good thoughts. Jokes help too.

1st chemo

Written Jan 10, 2013 4:04pm by Dave Robb

Finally picked my poison and started chemo today. Taking the latest and greatest meds.

I'm being treated at the Siteman Cancer Center. It's a big place. The waiting room is like an airport gate area and everyone gets a pager. When it's your turn they take you back to an area where there are 9 "pods." Each pod has about 6 patient bays. The whole place was full. It's a little overwhelming to see first-hand just how many people are facing their own battles.

They were unable to schedule me for a port, so we did today with an IV. Came in at 9AM, left a little after 3pm. Going forward it should be shorter - more like 4 hours. It will be one day a week for three weeks with one week off. Med levels will be reevaluated each week.

There was some trouble getting the IV in and one of the meds hurt slightly in the area of the IV - I am told that is not an issue once the port goes in next Tuesday.

Everyone has been very friendly so far - that helps.

Towards our new routine

Written Jan 16, 2013 8:07am by Dave Robb

Port went in yesterday. It went fast and was a surreal experience because they don't put you all the way out...or do they?

Anyway, since we were at the hospital and she had the availability, we finally connected with the dietician. It was after the port and I was completely stoned. Sabrina took good notes while I asked dumb questions like "what type of cookies can I eat?" and held forth on my appreciation of sparkling water.

Chemo again on Thursday.

Thanks to all for the messages, kind words, and the jokes.

Dave

Moving along

Written Jan 25, 2013 9:45am by Dave Robb

3rd chemo treatment yesterday. Trying to catch up on things today. I will be wiped out for the weekend and should start feeling better Monday. That has been the pattern so far. Next week I get a break! Perfect timing. It will be Sabrina's birthday and David & Diane Thurmond will be in town. Another one-month cycle and we will scan again to see what the tumor and lesions look like. Barring dramatic findings, there will most likely be another 2 month stretch of chemo and then a decision point on next steps. I am focusing on a few days at a time and will cross the next bridge when I get to it.

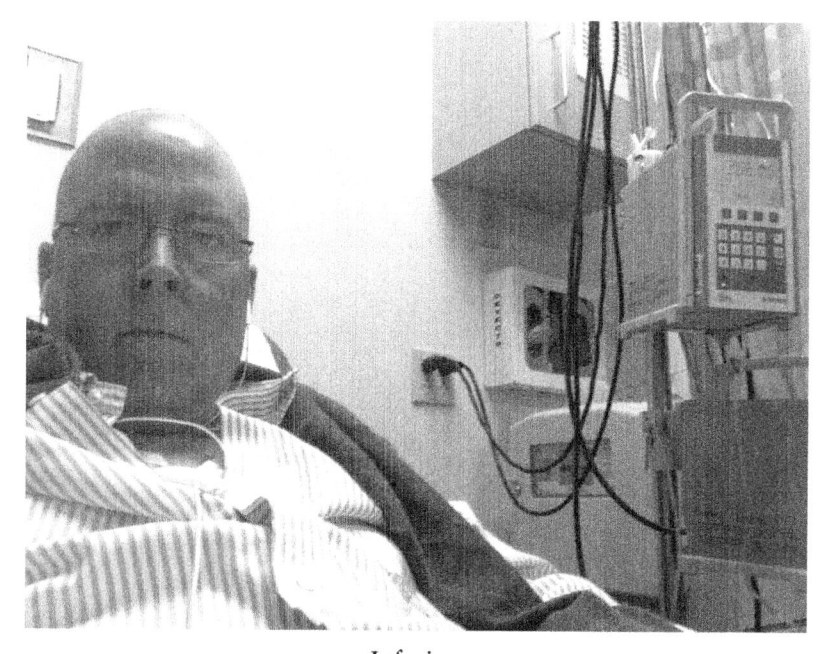

Infusion

Second Cycle

Written Feb 7, 2013 5:18pm by Dave Robb

2nd cycle of chemo began today. At the end of this month we'll scan again and see what the cancer looks like. Good news today is that liver numbers are back to normal and the oncologists continue to say that I am taking the chemo well.

Got home from the hospital and checked my mail. Received a quarterly usage/provider billings statement from the fine folks at the United Healthcare insurance company. Rack rate for all the care, test, scans, meds, and procedures billed in the last five weeks is more than $47,000. Glad I have insurance.

Regards,

Dave

Off to Texas

Written Feb 27, 2013 5:42pm by Dave Robb

On Monday we had a big meeting with the oncologist. I've completed two months of chemo and they did a new MRI to take a look at our progress.

The good news is that I haven't developed additional tumors and the ones I've got are not larger in size.

I shared this news with a friend who knows a thing or two about cancer and her response was "you say that as if there was some bad news." She is exactly right. This is good news...cancer style....but good news nonetheless.

So the plan for now is more of the same chemo mix.

Meanwhile, Sabrina and I leave tomorrow for MD Anderson in Houston to see if they have some other options for us to consider.

Not sure what kind of balloon animals they have down there but, hopefully, we'll come back with some entertaining photo updates.

Thanks to all for the notes, kind words, dinners, and love.

Balloon animals at Siteman Cancer Center

Back from Houston - now what?

Written Mar 6, 2013 1:20pm by Dave Robb

Trip to Houston went well. No easy answers or choices.

Our first visit to MD Anderson

Keeping an open mind

Written Mar 22, 2013 10:42am by Dave Robb

Sabrina and I are members of the Ladue Chapel Presbyterian Church. Unlike Sabrina, I do not attend very often. So when Sabrina scheduled a meeting Wednesday with one of our ministers, it was only at the last minute that I decided to tag along. I'm glad I went.

We talked about peace, the various meanings of healing, the faith of others, and - mostly with regard to my sons' well-being - the power of prayer.

Yes, this is actually Dave Robb writing this post! This is the 2nd time in two weeks that a revealing and meaningful moment has occurred seemingly by chance.

Meanwhile, it is a late winter in Saint Louis. I can't wait to see what Spring will bring for our garden and our sports court.

To all of those who have called, posted, etc., my apologies for not responding to you directly - time flows differently around here these days. Your messages are always appreciated.

On the medical front, all is calm. Chemo continues.

Love,

Dave

Time for some surgery

Written Apr 3, 2013 5:28pm by Dave Robb

We seem to be on a new and hopeful course. There is communication and cooperation occurring between the oncologists in Houston and STL and Sabrina and I are feeling very good that there appears to be a balance between the aggressive and conservative philosophies of the experts involved. We also have a surgeon here engaged - one of the best in the country for my situation.

The chemo I've been on for the last 3 months has kept me stable with very tolerable side effects - in fact, the latest MRI shows the liver mets shrinking. So, why abandon what is working? Because I cannot accept the prognosis that this is a near-term terminal illness. We MUST change longevity categories.

So here's the plan: move to FOLFIRINOX. This is a 5-drug combo that, like my current chemo, is fairly new. The data show it is typically more effective than what I'm on. Anecdotally, I'm told it has produced dramatic results for some people. The downside is that it is more toxic and with potentially worse side effects than I've become used to.

This Friday (April 5), I will go in for a laparoscopic surgery. The surgeon is going to take a look around my belly for cancer that may be hiding and not showing up on the scans.

The thinking is that if they find a mess in there, no need to put me through the more miserable chemo and, instead stay the current course for as long as possible. If all is clear, full ahead with FOLFIRINOX, which I will start in another week after surgery.

As a bonus on Friday, the surgeon may zap the larger liver lesion while he's in there. Hey, cancer, there's a whole lot more whoop-ass coming your way.

Love,

Dave

Dave in Recovery

Written Apr 5, 2013 10:10am by Sabrina Robb

Dave is out of surgery. There is no visible evidence of metastasis outside the liver! We are putting this in the good news category. The surgeon decided not to ablate the liver tumors so they can look forward to the Chemo whoop-ass Dave has planned for them in two weeks.

Dave and I continue to be overwhelmed by everyone's love and support and can't express how appreciative we are of our friends & family in St. Louis and afar. Thank you for constantly checking in, sending good thoughts and jokes, praying for us, feeding us, keeping Holden and Rhys engaged with playdates and keeping their lives as normal as possible, and for your offers to help in anyway. We are so thankful for the support we have and for all of you. Thank you to Dave's parents who are there whenever we need their help and ready to provide whatever we need. This is a challenging situation and your support gives us strength and encouragement. Thank you.

Sent from CaringBridge iPhone app

New chemo is in - feels different

Written Apr 19, 2013 2:24pm by Dave Robb

Started FOLFIRONOX, the new chemo regimen. Infusion day was Monday and it took the whole day due to the amount of meds (variety and volume). The new stuff comes with a couple of additional wrinkles:

First, I now have 46 continuous hours of home infusion. I leave the hospital with a pump and chemo bag in tow. It pumps away around the clock quietly chugging – just loud enough to remind me it's there (as if I had forgotten carrying it around in a shoulder bag). Infusion is a word I previously associated with steeping tea or aroma therapy – not pumping me full of toxic chemicals (the pump comes with its own "hazmat" cleanup kit and a 1-800 number for emergencies). Sabrina suggested that I give the pump a nickname. No problem, I gave it a nickname that she did not like and that I can't print here.

Second, one of the drugs carries an interesting side effect that makes me hyper-sensitive to cold (touching, drinking, eating, breathing).

My sons' curiosity with the pump has passed. And the other morning they both offered that their hands were not too cold for hugging. And Holden assured me his toys were warm enough for me to help pick-up.

So, between the pump, the cold sensitivity, and my bald head, I am feeling a bit like a comic book villain. Oh, and what little beard I have left has turned white. Maybe it is I who needs the nickname, not the chemo pump?

Lastly, special thanks to my brother, Aaron: for months, you have sat with me during many of my chemo-funk days. Lying in bed wiped out and dozing off periodically, I have not been a great companion - but you have. I love you.

Regards,

Dave

Captain Cold and his gang

Written Apr 28, 2013 2:37pm by Dave Robb

So, my comment about the comic book villain took on some energy.

First, my friend Gillian did some scholarly research and identified a bona fide comic book villain who seems to fit the situation: Captain Cold from DC Comics. He is a villain with a heart who lives by a moral code and whose powers have to do with ice beams, cold fields, and the ability to manipulate molecules.

My comic book nerd brother rightly pointed out that, with my cold sensitivity, that I should really be the opposite of Captain Cold, but I think the point is that I am stuck in a situation that is the exact opposite of where I want to be – so the paradox of Captain Cold is fine.

Next, Gillian and I looked at a variety of internet images to serve as my Captain Cold avatar. We narrowed it down to two. One is a classic retro comic book image. The other is a darker, graphic novel type.

We're putting it up for a vote. Which do you prefer? Please vote in the guestbook. I will probably find some copyright infringing uses for whichever image wins.

Meanwhile, our friends Jeff and Melissa and their daughters suggested that we should be seeking the help of super heroes, not villains, in our fight. To get us on the right track, they sent each of us home-made super hero capes! See the photo gallery. Thanks a million Powers family! Turns out the capes came imbued with the super power of creating a very entertaining Saturday night and transforming Rhys and Holden instantly into super heroes. Super heroes need villains, of course, so it seems "Captain Cold" is stuck as the villain for the moment.

FOLFIRINOX continues. 2 weeks down, 6 to go. Hitting the pump again Monday.

Love,

Dave

We can be who we need to be

Folfirinox is a frothy can of whoop-ass

Written May 3, 2013 1:38pm by Dave Robb

Thanks to everyone who shared input on the Captain Cold images. Looks like the graphic novel version won. Even if it was close, I had a tie-breaking experience at the hospital the other day.

After a full and nauseating day of infusion, we got into the car to go home and I suddenly experienced an intense pins-and-needles tingling in my hands, particularly my left hand with the tingling extending into my arm a bit, but the thing that really freaked me out was my hand cramping uncontrollably into a ball. Opening and closing my fist heightened the tingling sensation.

So, I felt very much like the winning Captain Cold image. Well, just the freezing fist and arm part, the rest of me felt like a scared, fragile cancer patient.

We walk back into the hospital and - because I have freaked myself out - my blood pressure is elevated and my chest a bit tight. This sets off a scramble: EKG, oxygen, blood work, allergy meds, observation. All is OK, no heart issue. More weird nerve-related stuff going on in the days since – we're working with the oncologists to figure this out.

Sabrina and I have learned that these detours are just a part of life in cancer treatment: the trip to the ER for swollen legs, tachycardia after a surgery, alarming liver enzyme spikes, and frozen hands. They come without warning – like turbulence during an airplane flight - and the doctors often don't have an exact explanation. I am coming to believe that, at moments like this, I am in God's hands. I am not clear in my understanding but now believe this to be more than just a figure of speech. There are also the talented, highly-trained hands of the staff at Siteman Cancer Center – somehow these hands are connected.

As always, there are too many people helping us to thank directly in this post. Here are just a few: Patience Schock for her healing soup and sage encouragement; Coco Bloomfield for the homemade granola; old friends Chip and Gabbi Paucek for making time for a leisurely lunch in the middle of their business trip to STL; Scott Cohn for reaching out and a great catch-up lunch; Lizzy's, Cole's, Kate's and John's families for the playdates; the anonymous Pizza Santa who had some gourmet pizzas delivered to our house; the nurses and techs in the treatment center for their hands-on compassion; and my parents again and again and again.

My next task is to identify a super hero avatar for Sabrina. In addition to taking care of me, our sons, and our business, she is dealing with some critical health issues with her mother, Anna. Any ideas? Remember that she already has a star-studded super hero cape – so that might figure into it, or not.

Lastly, some good news to report: more improvement on liver numbers, good white and platelet counts, and a tumor marker that continues to drop.

Folfirinox: 3 weeks down, 5 more to go. Then back to Houston.

Love,

Dave

More chemo

You Can't Un-ring the Cancer Bell

Written May 14, 2013 5:25am by Dave Robb

There is a nautical bell on the wall of the waiting area at the Siteman treatment center.

You walk by it on your way in and out. People ring it when they reach a major goal: clear scan, last chemo, etc. Everyone within earshot cheers and claps.

I'm pleased to say that I hear it ring every time I'm there. I'm happy for whoever is ringing the bell but, for me, it does stir mixed emotions. We'll get there.

Meanwhile, I think about the inscription below the bell: "Life is not measured by the number of breaths we take, but by the moments that take our breath away."

On the medical front: Folfirinox cycle 3 infusions began yesterday. After a lot of thought, discussion, and angst, the decision was made to omit irinotecan from this cycle. This is the drug that seems to have caused trouble previously. A swelling tongue is just too serious of a warning sign to simply try and power through. We will have an allergist do some testing with the idea of identifying a modification (pre-meds/dosage/etc.) to my treatment plan.

We also decided not to implement IV mineral supplements that are commonly used to help mitigate certain side effects of the oxaliplatin (which inhibits DNA synthesis in the cancer). There was a study that concluded that the supplements diminish the effectiveness of the drug. Then there was another study that concluded that the supplements don't reduce effectiveness. A contradiction, of course, right? But our STL oncologist put it well: "if we're treating you palliatively, the focus is on quality of life and comfort; if we're going for the cure, I'd hate to find out in the future that the first study was right." So, unless/until the side effects really get in the way, onward we go on that portion of the brew.

These were different decisions than I would make from the (also reasonable) suggestions from MD Anderson. That's why I'm so thankful to have a team in place with perspectives from both ends of the spectrum.

This entire process is full of these dilemmas. The doctors have deep and sophisticated (and incomplete) knowledge. Yet, I have to make my own decisions - with high stakes - based on their recommendations, logic, my goals, trust, and faith.

Sabrina says I have a love/hate relationship with my STL oncologist...and that he probably feels the same way.

Oh, and now my hair is growing back, go figure.

Love,

Dave

"Life is not measured by the number of breaths we take,
but by the moments that take our breath away."

Waiting for my chemo

Written May 22, 2013 9:12am by Dave Robb

On chemo day, I sit in a treatment station waiting for my chemo. It is one of 6 in a "pod." Some are beds and some are "armchairs." There are 9 pods on the floor. Fellow patients come and go as the hours pass.

The old woman across from me is newly diagnosed and sounds scared. Her cousin in Detroit has cancer, too. She tells her companion of the visions she is having. She struggles to understand what this all means.

The woman in the middle bed is a road warrior. She rolled in as if striding through a busy airport terminal – roller carry-on and all. She is on her cell phone, commanding other aspects of her cancer. Her companion is a part of the routine. They have gourmet snacks.

The kid is in his pajamas. Limbs and frame are locked stiff in the grip of his cancer. His companion could be his mother. She sits uncomfortably. They are silent. The nurse is on the phone with a Spanish translator: can't she just call back directly if there are more questions? No, she has to call the main number and start all over again.

An old couple enters, the wife takes her seat, the husband pulls up his chair. Her cancer is rendered invisible by their poise. They're sitting in a hotel lobby, or maybe church, or maybe just the same hospital as every other time. When they leave, the husband puts on his hat – the act of placing it reminds me of my grandfather.

The tattooed cowboy next to me leaves his boots on. "Back from Afghanistan on Friday, diagnosed with cancer on Monday!" It's been a long fight, but today is his last treatment: his cancer is beaten. He vanishes the moment the needle is withdrawn. Home to see his little girl.

Chemo day always awaits.

Milestones

Written Jun 4, 2013 8:11am by Dave Robb

During the darkest Winter days of January, as I recovered from my emergent liver illness and bile stent implant, and wrestled with the implications of my pancreas cancer diagnosis, I did not know how long I had to live. Still don't. Fact is, none of us know how much time we have.

But my future, or what I expected it to be, or what I thought I would ever eventually get around to figuring out what I wanted it to be, vanished. And I started to think of some very strange milestones that I feared I might miss. The big milestones were too painful to confront. So I focused on the small ones – because, I think, deep down I knew they, at least, would be achievable. Here are a few, they may seem trivial.

1. Skyfall. I missed this latest James Bond movie when it was in the theaters late last year. It was due on Cable On-Demand by mid-February. My brother and I watched it at my house. Spoiler alert: they brought Miss Moneypenny back! Nice touch.

My brother and I just saw another great movie the other day: Star Trek Into Darkness. First time I've been out to a theater in a while. We went to the Mosley's new theater downtown at the Mercantile Exchange. Stadium seating, tray tables, touchscreen tablets to order from the kitchen – how cool is that? Spoiler alert: there is a scene involving the warp drive reactor core – isn't there always in a Star Trek movie? The conversation between a mortally-irradiated Kirk and a helpless Spock got me all choked up. I get choked up a lot these days. It helps.

> 2. My sprinkler system. After months of planning, we installed an in-ground irrigation system last Fall and promptly shut it down for the season. I looked forward to having it opened in April, both as a harbinger of Spring and just to see the darn thing blow. The first day, I was up early (the meds). I followed the system around as it moved across 14 zones, first clockwise over the lawn and then counter clockwise to cover all the landscaping beds. It comes on around 3AM and runs about 5 hours.

On that first day, Rhys and Holden got up in time to see the bed zones. They were as excited as I to see each new set of spray heads pop up. By sunrise, it was a firework display of irrigation engineering. On nights I can't sleep, I sometimes wander around our yard and garden, following from zone to zone (these darn meds). The guys who deliver the newspaper must think I'm crazy standing there in my robe – crazier still if I am wearing one of my kimonos. Man those guys get up early to deliver those papers. Sometimes I'm inside writing these posts. It all helps.

> 3. Vampire Weekend came out with a new album in May. They are a favorite and I was eager and a little nervous to see what they'd come up with. And a mini-milestone: I finally bought an album in MP3 (still bought the CD version, too, though). It's a great album. Strangely, there is a mortality theme woven throughout. The music helps.

Turns out there have been many, many milestones over the past 5 months:

Our sons graduated from pre-school! So now we've got another milestone on the board: they'll start kindergarten in the Fall at my alma matter, Ralph M Captain Elementary School. I feel very lucky that we get to send our kids to school there. I plan to walk them to school on their first day – and many days thereafter.

Sabrina had a birthday, Valentine's Day passed, and so did Mother's day. I did my usual poor job of honoring any of these occasions. So, maybe these were milestones of normalcy. I love my wife very much.

My brother joined the Catholic Church and I was there, with our Mom and Dad, aunts/uncle, and cousins, to celebrate at the Easter Eve mass during which he was confirmed.

Aunts, an uncle, and many cousins have been to visit. Lots of yard games. More cousins on the way this month!

My dad had his own battle with cancer a couple of years ago. He recently had yet another clear check-up. In all this time he had never wrung the bell. He rode shotgun with me on a recent trip out to Siteman West – they have a bell out there, too. I encouraged him to ring it in celebration of his own milestones and even took a picture to document it. He's a tough and tender guy, my Dad.

And I am now a self-published author, I created two books: one for each of my sons. You can see the on-line previews at blurb.com

In our garden, our peonies bloomed, so did the spiderwort, the iris, and the crane's bill – the photos are in the gallery. The azaleas were very tired this year. But we had the biggest first blush yet for our roses. My big rhodo finally flowered after 3 years of dud buds. More to follow this season: hydrangea, lilies, astilbe, coreopsis, and others!

Off to Houston this week. Although I feel pretty good, my tumor marker number is not trending in the right direction (go ahead and google the crazy-making ambiguity of info on this topic or – better yet – don't). We'll just have to wait to see what the scans show. It is hard to wait. The milestones help.

Meanwhile, I see many of you enjoying your own successful milestones – small and large – and hope they are providing meaning and peace in your lives.

Love,

Dave

Knocking the tumors on their heels!

Written Jun 11, 2013 6:35am by Dave Robb

Went to Houston last week. Did the first scans since I've been on the FOLFIRINOX chemo regimen.

After an anxious weekend awaiting the doctors' opinions, we have received some amazing news.

For those keeping score: the largest liver tumor has shrunk from 1.3cm to 5mm. The other liver tumor has shrunk so much it was not visible on the scan. The last MRI had turned up a 3rd but it, too, is not showing up on the latest scan.

The pancreas tumor has shrunk from 2.3cm to 1.8cm.

This was a major crossroads in our roadmap. In addition to measurable success in fighting the tumors, this finding keeps the door open for pancreas tumor resection down the road.

Our Houston oncologist will be presenting my case again to the larger team at MD Anderson this week. We hope to hear soon what their thoughts are on next steps.

We'll circle back with the Siteman group this week and will look forward to their thoughts as well.

This was a big week.

Chemo again tomorrow. Still some scary stuff, but a lot less so knowing that it is working.

We have been crying tears of joy and gratitude.

Love,

Dave

Funny Story

Written Jun 27, 2013 11:36am by Dave Robb

I have always respected pharmacists and believe the majority to be hardworking, compassionate people. To do their job well, they require a unique combination of skills that probably few people can muster consistently.

Unfortunately for me, the closest Walgreens is a high-volume affair with mostly junior pharmacy staff. If Bravo Network (and fellow CHS-alum Andy Cohen) were going to produce a reality show about pharmacies, they might film it here.

Recently, I was heading into a 24 hour period where I was going to be taking some new meds in a large combination with others. I thought I should ask the pharmacist about this.

Me: "I haven't taken this combination of meds before, can you please take a look at all this? Anything I should be on the lookout for?"

Pharmacist: "Wow, these are a lot of drugs."

Me (dumbfounded): "Yes….that's why I'm asking about it."

Pharmacist: "These are really going to knock you out. Does your doctor know you are taking all this?"

Me: "Um…you filled the prescriptions."

Pharmacist: "Well, I guess they must want you knocked out for whatever is going to happen."

Me (regretting asking): "Yeah....for whatever is going to happen....thank you."

After all the "whatever was going to happen," we went for a quick trip to the lake. Rhys and Holden got to put this year's swimming lessons to work and had a blast splashing in the lake and swimming in the pool (photos in the gallery).

Met with the STL surgeon Monday. He is of the same opinion as Houston at the moment: continue on with the FOLFIRINOX chemo for a while and see what further response we can achieve. He continues to hold the door open for surgery - and that is the path we need to stay on.

Although we always leave his office feeling hopeful and strong, the cold hard truth is that this surgeon has only ever had one patient with my set of issues that has survived long-term (8 years out). This guy is one of the best in the country and has been at it a long time, so I figure he is due for another long-term survivor story to share with his future patients.

Lastly, I spoke with a fellow pancreas cancer fighter the other day. He relayed a quote he had read about the three things you need to win the fight: "someone to love, something to do, and something to look forward to." I'm thankful to have a lot of each of these three. And I think these are the things we all need.

Hope your summer is off to a great start.

Love,

Dave

Summertime, swimming, dishwashers, & more chemo

Written Jul 16, 2013 9:01am by Dave Robb

I woke up in the middle of the night from a series of dreams. They were random dreams where I was in a variety places with the mix of unexpected characters that I enjoy in my dreams.

It had been a rough week and a bad few days. But, despite it being 4 am, the moment I woke up I could tell I was feeling better. I don't think I had dreamed in days.

We're pretty far into the FOLFIRINOX chemo. And it's getting a little tougher lately. The oncologist tells me we're past the point where they often have to start suspending treatment or reducing dosages. We've seen the counts start to drop a bit, but they can be "normal" one day and low the next. So far, though, we've been moving at full speed.

It's hard to describe what it feels like. The old stuff was easier to describe: it felt like having a case of the flu for three-four days out of every seven. Some cycles were worse than others.

The FOLFIRINOX is more evanescent. I've written previously about the neurotoxicity. That seems to be under control, at least as far as something called "neurotoxicity" can be under control, right? Believe it or not, hiccups appear to be an occasional side effect and there is often a bad taste in my mouth and my head hurts.

And, if you really want to know about it, you can ask Sabrina about the gas…the horror….

The thing that is a challenge lately is being tired and feeling weak. My neighbor says that is just a "preview of getting old," so I will try to keep it in perspective.

I have been in bed more with a listless fatigue. And I've briefly run a fever the week following each of the last three infusions. The fevers are unpleasant but have only resulted in one trip, so far, to the hospital…which was memorable for having met "the worst nurse at Barnes Hospital."

Sabrina suggests that the fevers could be my body reacting to the tumor tissue as it passes from the body. I like to think that she's right. It is as helpful a thought as anything the doctors have offered.

So this is an endurance part of our journey. Chemo day comes around ready or not. Another difference of this regimen is that chemo day itself is very rough. Sometimes I cry in the car during the drive to the hospital, sometimes I curse like a sailor. You have to get ready for feeling sick. I'm never quite sure what it will bring – this week it was sharp pain in my knees. Infection? Swelling? Knee cancer? Who knows what it was. I feel better today.

Then there's the other challenge, the fear comes around ready or not. I'm going in for scans a month early. I have to wait for the appointment and then I'll have to wait for the findings.

I believe we are beating this cancer. I believe the scans will show success.

The waiting is hard; you have to put the fear out of your mind.

And then my dishwasher breaks. So there I am at Lowes, buying a dishwasher. Declining an extended warranty and paying too much for installation. My sons are at the pool. They each jump off the diving board for the first time. Sabrina catches the magic on her iPhone.

Love,

Dave

One day at a time

You meet a lot of people along the way.

Written Jul 26, 2013 10:44am by Dave Robb

You meet a lot of people along the way.

I sat next to a fellow pancreas cancer patient and his wife the other day. He has a different situation than mine – a worse one. Like us, they've travelled across the country to seek out alternatives. His options have narrowed and it sounds as if he is now on a truly palliative path. We were both in for chemo: he had just switched from my current regimen to my old regimen. His cancer had recently progressed, so it was time to switch chemo. "Progression" and "progressed" are bad words in one's cancer fight – it means your tumors are growing or that the cancer is spreading. His progression had triggered some serious internal bleeding leading to a week in the ICU.

So, here this guy is, the very next week, back in the saddle on his new chemo. He's been fighting for 1.5 years and has a great attitude. He values his exercise and feels grateful for his time. He's happy to be off the FOLFIRINOX because it messed with his taste buds and everything tasted bad to him. Now here's a man who looks for the silver linings: the guy nearly exsanguinates, and he's looking forward to tasting good food again!

As we were enjoying our conversation, and as I was about 30 minutes into the "back-nine" of chemo day, I hit an unexpected reaction to the oxaliplatin: a sudden rash on my hands, face, and neck. Infusion halted, steroids and Benadryl administered, held for observation. The oxaliplatin is the stuff that makes me cold-sensitive, so it looks like I'll get a break on that this cycle. I'm going to take a page from my new friend's book and find the silver lining: it's Milkshake Day! We'll figure out the adjustments needed for the next cycle. Just another detour on our march forward.

I think I was more frustrated than scared this time, because we ARE moving forward and we ARE succeeding. Got scanned early last week. They stuck me in their latest and greatest MRI tube...one of only two in the state of Missouri. Only one liver tumor is currently visible. This is a 2nd scan with this finding, so that it very encouraging. CT of the chest. Between the two, no visible signs of further mets.

And the technician somehow has the MRI hooked up to Pandora Internet Radio and offered to make me whatever station I wanted to listen to (it's about a 40 minute scan). I chose Thievery Corporation.

My sons are sick this week and had to miss the performing arts camp and the water park, but I think they've turned the corner in time for church camp next week. Sabrina's mom is back in the hospital – it is amazing how Sabrina keeps this whole ship afloat. I heard Carnival Cruiselines was looking for new management, maybe it's time for a career change!

Love,

Dave

Back to school, back to Houston

Written Aug 20, 2013 9:17am by Dave Robb

The worst part: "The worst part" of living with cancer is the constant fear that you have not yet gotten to "the worst part" of living with cancer.

Finding out you have cancer: Doctors do a terrible job of telling you that you have cancer. I've listened to other people's stories and am living my own. It's not like the movies. For me, there was not a dramatic scene where the doctor broke the news with carefully chosen words while sitting in a comfortable office. Rather, there was a process of elimination and discovery as we tried to figure out what was going on – I think this is probably the more common experience. So, instead of the big reveal, there were actually a series of meetings (in exam rooms, clinic vestibules, and recovery areas) as we peeled back the layers of the onion. In my case, there were about 5 meetings with 4 different doctors and the news was worse each time. I listened to what they said but it took at least a month before I could "hear" it. Sabrina heard it all right away.

As the fight moves forward, these meetings become a part of the routine. There is good news, there is forward movement, but there are always caveats.

Hope: People like to say "kids are resilient." They say this to be reassuring, but I'm not convinced. Kids don't have a fully developed sense of fear or judgment – so, perhaps we mistake this for resilience. When it comes to my sons, I can tell you that this cancer is rocking their world…hard. But I can also tell you, beyond any doubt, that my sons have hope. They operate daily from a deep, innate well of pure, golden hope. The hope can get us to resilience.

Faith: We were in Houston again this week to see the doctors there. In between appointments, we stopped in at the hospital chapel. As I sat silently contemplating my sons' hopefulness, Sabrina handed me a bible and pointed to a passage from Hebrews 11 that had been a reading at last Sunday's service back home:

"Now faith is confidence in what we hope for and assurance about what we do not see."

This is such a great definition of faith and it also gets to the heart of fighting metastatic disease. The fear and doubt, looming failure, the monster lurking in the dark is what we can't see. It is the micro-metastasis that may or may not be close by or travelling the far-flung reaches of my body. In other words, what we do not see is "the worst part."

Indolence: Sabrina was surprised and perhaps secretly amused to discover that the CT scan picks up a picture of "the full Monty."

The great news is that none of the previously visible liver mets are visible in this scan. The bad news is that there is a small shadow that the radiologist thinks could be a new met. If it is a new met, then the chemo has yielded a mixed response and we have hit a roadblock.

How do we find out? After 7 straight months of chemo, I get to take a break! We'll let some time pass and then take another look at the liver. If nothing comes of this new spot, we'll be on to the next step, which may be chemo-radiation therapy on the pancreas.

As I've written about before, "progress" is a bad word in the bizarro world of cancer. But it turns out that "indolent" is actually a good word. As in: "during your chemo break, your indolent pancreas cancer did not progress."

As I get my strength back in the coming weeks, I hope to be very productive and use my time wisely. To my cancer, on the other hand, I say: "have a nice break you lazy, greedy monster...we'll be seeing you this Fall with a whole new arsenal of whoop-ass."

Love,

Dave

First day of Kindergaarten, Rhys is ready to ride

Here comes the radiation!

Written Sep 13, 2013 1:09pm by Dave Robb

Holden said something this morning that made my day: "Daddy, you're not sick, you just have cancer."

Nurses routinely run through a checklist of symptoms and side effects with me. Early on, the checklist felt sort of unnecessary: questions about nausea (sometimes), pain (sometimes), numbness/tingling (yes, a lot), diarrhea (occasionally), constipation (yup), off-balance (not in a while), dizziness (not really, but maybe with the pain pills), and the list goes on…. The farther I've journeyed, the more boxes have been checked – at least occasionally – so I now have a better appreciation of the questions. I'm pleased to report I have not fallen over and that I am still able to button a button (which is good because my PJ bottoms and some of my underwear have a button fly…TMI?). Seriously though, I'm doing pretty well. Like Holden says, I'm not sick, I just have cancer.

It's been 5 weeks since my last infusion and it is great to have a break from the chemo. I am slowly catching up on some chores around the house. The other weekend I went on-line to research how to extend the WIFI range in our house to serve our ever-expanding array of wireless gadgets. I found all sorts of information and solutions. And, most helpfully, I read detailed user reviews on some of the products that held the most promise.

That same weekend, I went on-line to research the neo-adjuvant chemo radiation therapy prior to pancreas resection. I found a handful of abstracts of research papers written about studies at various teaching hospitals around the world. Most were inconclusive. Those that weren't, did not really answer the fundamental question I have about this topic. There were no user reviews. I also ended up on a couple of the cancer support discussion boards – any attempt at on-line cancer research can easily leave you washed up on those rocky shores.

Over the months, I've happened across a handful of blogs about families and their stage four pancreas cancer journeys. The blogs follow a familiar arc. Someone is healthy and unsuspecting. They get sick and discover it's cancer. These blogs might be written by the cancer patient or their spouse, or sometimes there are contributions from both. They are initially shocked by the diagnosis. Chemo starts. Maybe there is some surgery mixed in there somewhere. The chemo works and the tumors shrink and the good news is blogged about. The chemo works until it doesn't, and then there is new chemo. There are complications and hospital stays. And pain. Pain of all kinds. And then the physical pain is medically managed. The posts alternate between those about medical details and those about the family's journey. The family holds it together with the help of loved ones and their faith. Over time, the body continues to betray the family in increasingly grotesque ways. At some point, the posts come only from the spouse. The blog goes quiet for a while. Then comes the post that the end has become inevitable. A short while later comes the post that the fight is over.

I don't mean to be dismissive or disrespectful to these brave families by making the above generalization and summary, but these really are the stories of pancreas cancer that you see. Their blogs do provide an example of how to live with grace, fight with courage, and love without limit. I am deeply thankful for being physically comfortable, for the stability of my disease, and success we are achieving towards our big, outrageous goal. But if you're looking for encouragement and a guide to the cure – you're not going to find it on-line. Nor will you find it among your doctors – at least not enough to get you there. The will to do what I need to do is an individual affair with the support of my loved ones and all of those that have taken an interest and offered their support.

We've sought the opinions of the smartest people on the planet when it comes to pancreas cancer and, to be frank, we're operating based on educated guesses and professional instinct at this point.

After the last trip to Houston and 3 more weeks of meetings here and a fresh MRI, we've arrived at a tenuous consensus about the next step: chemo radiation therapy on the pancreas tumor.

I'll know more next week, but it will go something like this. They will perform a surgical procedure to place a marker on (in/around???) my pancreas tumor. This marker will allow them to shoot the radiation more accurately at the tumor without collateral damage (their words) to surrounding tissue/organs. I guess if I sneeze in the middle of being irradiated, the equipment somehow follows the marker. There is a comedy sketch in there somewhere but I'm just not feeling it today.

The "zapping" will occur each weekday for 6 weeks. Each week I will also be given a full dose of gemcitabine (a chemo drug – which I finally spelled correctly today without looking it up). The idea is that the radiation will do some damage to the primary tumor and, hopefully, prevent it from throwing out any new cancer (if it is indeed still doing this – no way to tell). And the systemic chemo – although not as potent as either of the regimens I was on this year – will hopefully provide some benefit in regards to potential metastasis and the remaining liver lesion. It will take a few weeks to get this all planned and in place.

Meanwhile, the Great Forest Park Balloon Race and the Saint Louis Scottish Games and Cultural Festival are coming up in the next couple of weeks. We live right across the street from the venue for both of these. Should be fun!

Love,

Dave

They gave me tattoos!

Written Sep 30, 2013 10:44pm by Dave Robb

This is another one of those weeks. I am waiting for scans at the end of the week that will - once again - determine my future path: no metastasis and we move forward to radiation, new mets and we're back to systemic chemo and moving sideways.

I'm counting on moving forward. Last week we completed the implantation of fiducial markers in my pancreas tumor and underwent a "simulation" where they scanned to map out my gut from which they will make their calculations, etc., on where and how long to shoot the radiation. They also molded a "cradle" that I'll lay in to help keep me still. They also marked up my torso in three places. It is a treasure map of sorts, marking how to find my pancreas tumor and the gold buried there (literally...the fiducials are made of gold).

There are permanent tattoos under the pen marks and tape! It helps them shoot the radiation at the right spot. I picture Sean Connery in The Hunt for Red October: "Hey, Ryan, be careful what you shoot at. Most things in here don't react well to bullets."

I'm a little nervous about the radiation, so I'm getting specific about the questions I am asking at the hospital, like: "are you sure there is no issue with radiation and the solastic polymer coating on the WallFlex cover on my biliary stent?" And today I called with some instructions for the radiologist that I wanted added to the radiation oncologist's MRI order. Yup, they're really getting to know me in the radiation oncology department. Thankfully, for them, this part will only last about six weeks.

They gave me a tour of the room where they administer the radiation. It is behind a giant metal "blast door." The machine is the most far-out, Star Wars-looking piece of equipment I have yet to see. And for some reason, the technicians did not bother to turn off the green positioning lasers that were beaming all around the room. I felt like we might be on a James Bond-style assignment to steal the chip out of the radiation machine.

So, while we wait: this weekend in Saint Louis is **Pedal the Cause**. It is an amazing cancer research fundraising event with 100% of contributions going to cancer research at The Siteman Cancer Center (where I'm being treated) and St. Louis Children's Hospital. As many of you know, Sabrina is riding 50 miles on Sunday. She is a part of a team of friends and work colleague's that will roll Sunday as "Robb's Riders." Rhys and Holden are doing the 1 mile kids' ride on Saturday. There is still time to support this worthy cause. To the many of you who have already been so generous with your contributions – thanks very much.

Love,

Dave

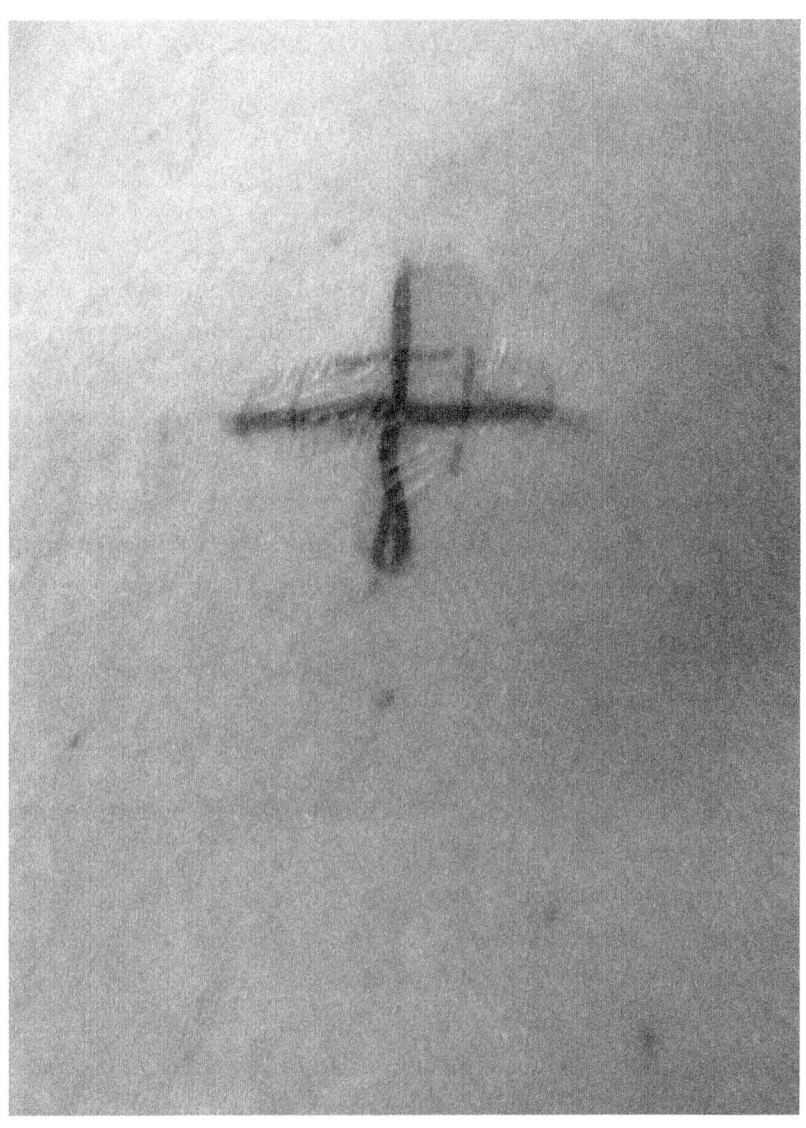

Ready…aim…

LIVING BETWEEN THE SCANS | 51

Hair, photons, and an amazing ride

Written Oct 14, 2013 6:44pm by Dave Robb

I am standing in my bathroom over the weekend looking in the mirror. Last week was the first week back in treatment; there's been chemo, 4 radiation sessions, and lots of supporting drugs. I look at the rash on my face, it is blistered more than usual and I wonder if the Elidel cream will continue to keep it in check with the new therapy. I look at my eyes, they are glassy from all the drugs. Checking my skin tone for any signs of jaundice, any chance that stent is clogging? And I look at my hair and wonder if it will fall out again.

My son walks in. He sees me staring at myself in the mirror searching for signs of my health. Searching for myself.

When I lost my hair earlier this year, it was upsetting because it was a constant reminder of the severity of my situation and the loss of control over my own body...and life. Wake up in the morning, stumble into the bathroom, pee (with all the meds I go for an eternity), load up the toothbrush, look in the mirror...yeah, I still have cancer. The hair loss was upsetting for my sons, too. And when the hair started to come back, it was, to them, a cause for celebration. In their mind, hair meant I was getting better and that meant: life going back to normal.

So, throughout the year, my hair has been a topic of concern, speculation, and amusement in our household.

They say that when your hair comes back, it comes back different. That's been true for me: it is wavier, thinner, and a slightly different color – just slightly. I sported a beard for a while – never had one of those before, so why not give it a try? When I shaved it off, I had to explain to my sons that it was just a matter of preference and nothing to worry about.

One of the things they don't specifically warn you about before chemo is that the hair falls out everywhere. Yup, everywhere.

Being bald is one thing, but not having eyebrows and eyelashes – that's the tell. People look at you funny. I don't think they mean to be rude. In fact, I don't think it's deliberate at all. There's just an uncanniness to it and people pick up on it: hmm, that guy must be sick.

When you don't have eyelashes, the tears don't well up in your eyes. There is nowhere for them to pause before streaming down your face. And no hair in your nose? Carry a tissue, it gets all watery, like a dog's nose.

So, my hair has been back for months and I'm standing in my bathroom looking in the mirror and having a really shitty moment. And then my son walks in and tells me I look good. "One day soon, Dad, your gonna have so much hair, your beard's going to be just like Pop-pop's and Uncle Aaron's." I think my eyelashes caught the tears before he could see them. But it doesn't matter if he did.

The chemo radiation therapy is going well. I go in every weekday and lay on a platform next to an enormous machine (a linear accelerator). The machine has parts that stick out and rotate around me 360 degrees. The machine shoots me with photons. Yup, photons. They would not let me take a photo of the actual machine – something about patient privacy (um? I'm the patient?) – so it makes the whole thing even more mysterious.

There is a CD player in the room with a limited library of disks. So far it has mostly been Frank Sinatra and Bob Marley. The other day I made the mistake of letting them put on a classical music CD. As I lay there on the platform I had a flashback of the Edward G Robinson euthanasia scene from the sci-fi movie Soylent Green. All I could think of was "get me out of here." That, and "Soylent Green is made of....PEOPLE!!!" Today they played an Eagles CD. Much better.

Lastly, thanks to everyone for their support of Pedal the Cause fundraising ride. Sabrina completed her 50 mile ride and Rhys and Holden participated in the children's ride. It wasn't until afterwards that we did the math and realized Rhys had ridden 10 miles! Together, the Dielmann Sotheby's "Robb's Rider's" team finished among the top 10 fundraisers in the corporate challenge division. That's a cohort that includes the likes of Edward Jones Investments, Stifel Financial, Emerson, and other STL corporate titans. Way to go team! And way to go friends! Special thanks Stephanie Oliver, Sarah Tadlock, Heather Johnson, the rest of the riding team and many others in the Dielmann crew for their time, spirit, and spectacular results!

Love,

Dave

Fundraising for cancer research

Ringing the Raydonkulous Bell

Written Nov 20, 2013 10:30am by Dave Robb

Last week I rang the bell.

It was the final radiation session in my chemo radiation therapy. Due to the science, you can only do one series of radiation treatments on this organ – there's no going back. So I felt like the bell was warranted.

The radiation portion was managed by a radiation oncologist. They call these guys "Rad-Onc" (pronounced ray-donk). This is different from the medical oncology folks (Med-Onc) who handle the chemo. The Rad-Onc group is a little bit of a different breed. For starters, they keep them down in the basement with no windows along with their multi-million dollar radiation machines. Legend has it that the bell tradition got its start down in Rad-Onc. People liked it, so they put a bell upstairs in the chemo treatment center.

The hope is that the radiation has killed the pancreas tumor and that there are no active cancer cells in that tumor. Unfortunately, there is no way to know for certain. The only known "cure" for my disease is a very big surgery called the Whipple Procedure which is what we have been driving toward all year. The irony is that if we've killed the tumor with radiation, we won't know until it is removed during the Whipple (along with parts of my pancreas, stomach, gallbladder, intestine, and some other things), in which case the Whipple, in one way of looking at it, will have been unnecessary.

Some people might call it a Catch-22:

> Yossarian: "That's some catch, that Catch-22"
>
> Doc Daneeka: "It's the best there is…"
>
> Me, I call it raydonkulous.

The week before was the final chemo infusion as a part of this therapy. The final dose was reduced due to a low count in the blood. First time we've had a low count that has altered a dosage. However, I had agreed with the Siteman team to go for the "Michigan" dose throughout this therapy; this is two to three times larger than what they give you at MD Anderson. So, even with the reduction, it was more than a full dose would have been in Houston. The chemo and radiation work synergistically.

My weight is steady (I've put a on a number of pounds since the FOLFIRINOX ended). However, as I was told to expect, I am fatigued. This should persist for a while. I'm told it may be months before we see the full response to this therapy. I am also experiencing some pain in my stomach and back and am taking more pain medicine than usual. It also appears that a small area on my back has been "burned" by the radiation. It was probably the place on my body where the pancreas was the closest to the surface in the field of treatment.

So here's the plan: sit tight and enjoy the holidays, scans on Dec 30, and meet with med-onc and rad-onc on Dec 31. The med-onc wants to scan earlier to look for mets. The compromise is we'll continue to monitor the tumor marker and scan if it spikes (it has been low – even normal – lately).

If things look good on the 31st, this may be the beginning of the long wait. If I can demonstrate stability (no progression) for many months, then we get the Whipple.

Love,

Dave

Finally ringing the bell!

Cancer – Year Two

Written Jan 6, 2014 3:44pm by Dave Robb

I hope everyone is off to a great start so far this year.

It's been a while since I've written. Chemo Radiation wrapped up mid-November and it's been great to have a break and enjoy the holidays and let the focus be the "normal" parts of our lives. Cancer World is never far away or without fire drills, however, so we did have a detour to look at my gallbladder for gallstones. Except for some sludge (their term), everything is OK in there. And if we make it to our audacious goal of the Whipple procedure, my gallbladder will be history anyway.

We scanned last week – first time since October 3rd. We could have scanned sooner but, if it turned up bad news, there was no point in ruining Christmas – so I decided to wait. I've been meaning to write about IV placement (they need one for contrast dye on certain scans) – there's a whole post to be explored on that topic but let's save it for another time.

So the scan came back with two spots suspicious for new cancer. Had to wait a week for the tumor board to meet and review. Cancer World has a lot of wait-and-see and that can be harder than being on therapy, where at least you feel like you are actively fighting. Anyway, the call came in this morning and the consensus is that the spots are not new mets (most likely). Turns out this was a really great scan: all of the tumors that they have been tracking for the last year have shrunk.

Surgery is on the table, and maybe sooner rather than later. In fact, I think the surgeon wants to get in there while he can still see the liver tumors! Better to go now and get them, than do the rest of the surgery and leave invisible cancer in the liver. This is balanced against waiting a little longer after the last therapy to see if new mets declare themselves.

We travel to Houston tomorrow to check in with the folks there. We want to gather as much consensus as possible on the advisability of surgery and timing.

I am so grateful for where we are that I struggle with what to do with this gratitude. There is so much to be done this year.

Meanwhile, Rhys lost his first tooth yesterday. There was a big snow storm here yesterday and the tooth fairy did not come. Oops! Must have been the snow (rough on the wings).

Love,

Dave

It's Whipple Time!

Written Jan 10, 2014 3:33pm by Dave Robb

This was a big week. My case was reviewed again by the tumor board at Siteman, we made a trip to Houston to see the pancreas wizard, and had a meeting yesterday with the surgeon here in St. Louis. Two amazing things have happened: (1) there seems to be more consensus on my case than there has ever been and (2) I'm scheduled for the big surgery on February 4th.

This is it. A shot at the only proven "cure." Historically, they don't do this surgery for stage 4 guys like me but the science is moving forward, we've had great support, our excellent medical team has done their best, we've fought hard for it, and many prayers have been answered to deliver us to this moment.

I will try to write again with details before the big day but, if I don't, the next journal post may be from Sabrina saying that I'm in recovery.

Love,

Dave

Waiting

Written Jan 22, 2014 8:12pm by Dave Robb

I was so excited to share our news in the last post that I neglected to write about some other thoughts I had from the last trip to Houston.

Our routine is to have a car service meet us in arrivals. On the latest trip, an extra bag road along in our car; another family had just arrived and was heading to the same destination and was carrying an enormous amount of luggage, more than would fit in their car. Our drivers were parked next to each other, so the extra bag rode with us. There are people who travel from all over the country; many undergo treatment or surgery in Houston, so they and their families make an extended stay. I am so thankful to have the option of treatment and surgery at Siteman, it is very healing to be at home and not in another city. Many of the hotel's rooms have kitchenettes, there is a coin-operated laundry room, and, on this trip, I noticed that a fellow guest on our floor – presumably dissatisfied with the in-room coffee maker – had purchased a Tassimo machine (the empty box was in the hall). They must be settling in for a long stay.

We've refined the logistics over the past year and pack lightly. On arrival day I opt to have labs drawn at the hotel, there is actually a little satellite location off the lobby and it's much more convenient than walking across the bridge to have them drawn in the hospital. There's a bit of a wait and I sit in the lounge room across from the blood place. I strike up a conversation with the fellow sitting next to me. He, too, has his routine down to a science; his visits are structured in the precise manner that frequent flyers plan their most travelled routes. This is his 3rd year of travelling to MD Anderson and he is finally in monitoring mode and has now made the transition from 3 month check-ins to 6 month check-ins. He's in his 60's and lives in New Mexico. Turns out we have connections to many of the same cities and talked about our travels. Strangely, we don't talk about cancer. We talk about grilling; after years of experimentation, he claims to have mastered the rack of lamb.

Sabrina and I decide to grab a quick bite to eat at the hospital cafeteria, which is a lot less expensive than the hotel and offers some reasonably healthy options. As we walk down one of the endless corridors, there is a teen-aged girl walking toward us. She is walking with a companion – must be her sister. Because she is wearing shorts, I can see that her left leg, below her knee, is gone. Its replacement is a bionic-looking engineering solution wrought of metals and plastics. She walks with an even gate. No limp, no struggle with its weight, no jerky motion in articulation with her knee. She has very nice posture. She is pretty.

Over the past year, I have encountered many people who are missing things: legs, jaws, chins, cheeks, breasts, and various bits, wedges, and segments. Cancer will take a lot from you. Most of what it takes may not be visible to others: energy, longevity, your confidence, your sense of safety, plans for your future, money, relationships, your sense of yourself. Or maybe it won't take these things from you, maybe it will just test you and wrestle with you – using the dirtiest and cruelest of tricks - pushing you as far towards breaking as you will go. On February 4th, cancer will take my digestive system. The surgeons will recreate it in a different fashion.

What I have learned over the past year is that in place of what the cancer takes, life offers gifts. It's not one-for-one. It's not a fair or even trade. But there are gifts. I don't think that they are earned; rather, I believe, that if you listen and if you open your mind and ease your grip, you might be able to receive a few gifts that would never have otherwise been available to you. Some people call these gifts blessings, some call it God's grace.

As we wait in the GI department for our appointment, Sabrina and I each, separately, see a man in a wheelchair. He might be my age, maybe younger, and is emaciated and slumped uncomfortably in his chair. A freshly rinsed emesis basin (barf bucket) rests in his lap – it looks like he might be needing it again soon. I am thankful for my health and a shot at the cure.

As we leave our appointment, another couple who arrived in the department around the same time as us, waits next to us for the elevator. It is obvious that their meeting has not gone as well as ours: her face is cast in shocked despair. And so it goes, all day, any day, all over this place in which we've found ourselves.

I am very scared about what lies ahead but I envision myself on the other side of this: cured, healthy, eating and exercising with thought and discipline, continuing to re-prioritize, looking for ways to give back, exploring the blessings. I envision going to the lake with my wife and sons. I envision the enormous scar that I will carry on my abdomen: it will be an inverted V, depending on the access the surgeons decide they need. "V for victory" Sabrina says.

A member of the surgeon's team described the scar shape as a chevron. There's something I like about that, something empowering. Yes, a chevron. I have been given the chance to earn that and I am grateful.

Love,

Dave

Awaiting the flight home from Houston

Whip the Cancer with a Whipple!

Written Feb 4, 2014 2:08pm by Sabrina Robb

Dave is out of surgery! The Dr. indicated that everything went very well – so well he could not find any cancer cells! The two lesions in the liver could not be located to ablate. The primary tumor in the pancreas did not show any cancer cells. This is an amazing response to the chemo & radiation therapies. Now the recovery period begins followed by most likely 6 more months of chemo therapy to kill any single microscopic cancer cell that may have gotten through the past therapies and surgery. This surgery brings Dave's chances of long term survival (5 years after diagnosis) from 1% to about 25%! I see many more wonderful years together in our future! Can't wait to share the news with Dave – he is still in recovery:)

Thanks so much for the outpouring of love, support and prayers. There are so many of you that have made this last year tolerable. Thank you.

More updates at a later time...

Footprints In the Sand

As you can see from the time and date stamp on the post below, I wrote this one much later. A year into the future, in fact. So, unlike the other chapters in this book, this one appears out of the chronological order in which it was written. It is a pivotal moment, so it makes sense to appear here to better understand what comes after.

I started to write this post many times, but never was able to figure out what I wanted to say or how to say it. Usually, the act of writing these posts is therapeutic. Even if there is not satisfaction, there is at least catharsis in the act of publishing the post. In the process of writing or the act posting, there is often some lesson that I learn, some insight or relief.

Nothing felt good about writing this entry. Noting felt good about posting it. But a couple of days later, I was reminded – really out of nowhere – of the poem "Footprints In the Sand." I looked it up on-line and read the poem again for the first time in decades.

For me, the Whipple and the time in the hospital that followed, were a part of the journey where there was only a single set of footprints.

One Year Cancer Free

Written Feb 4, 2015 7:15am by Dave Robb

Feel free to skip this one. I am writing this mostly to get it out of my head

Today, it is one year since my Whipple surgery. For a while now I've dwelled on it more than I would like: the surgery, my hospital stay, and the time that followed.

In the warped calculus of pancreatic cancer, it was truly a small price to pay; many never get the chance. But among the continuing costs are thoughts and emotions that seem to have become permanent, just like the fundamental changes to my anatomy that the surgeons made deep in my gut. In fact, these things seem to have embedded themselves in my gut. I feel them there.

Hard to believe it has been a year, some parts of it are so vivid in my memory's eye, that it seems much more recent. Some parts are growing increasingly vague. But it has been a year. Nearly 40,000 more people in the United States have died of pancreatic cancer during that time.

I'm not certain of the medical accuracy of anything I'm writing here. My recollection of the Whipple is purely how I experienced it. And I experienced it through a lens of pain, anxiety, sleep and food deprivation, and a lot of medication.

The whole thing starts the day before with no solid food after lunchtime. In the evening I begin a bowel cleanse process that involves drinking a "tonic" followed by rumbling in my belly, followed by continuous visits to the toilet for the next 10 hours.

The next morning, the day of surgery, we arrive around 5:30AM at the hospital. In our case, this is a major regional medical center. There is a large waiting room - a series of rooms, really. We arrive just as the doors open for the day but somehow there are already people inside.

The waiting area reminds me of a series of airport gates: families sitting with their carry-on luggage and some with pillows. We check in and are given a pager, the kind you might be given at a chain restaurant. There are young men wearing jackets and ties. They are pages of some sort, I'm not really sure what their role is.

When the pager goes off, we go back to the front desk and are directed to an elevator. We walk back through all of the waiting areas. To the very back, to a small elevator door. It is an Alice in Wonderland experience. We take the elevator to the designated floor. When we get off, there is an endless, windowless, harshly lit corridor. There are stripes on the floor of different colors. An attendant tells us which color to follow. The stripe leads us to a large preparation area.

In the prep area, we are greeted by a nurse and taken to a bay, given a large clear plastic bag, and instructed to remove all clothes and belongings and place them in the bag. I am given a gown and socks to wear. There may also have been an elastic-rimmed cap.

The nurse asks lots of questions, which always mildly irritates me because it is all in the computer already. I'm given an ID bracelet and an allergy bracelet.

There are some liability waivers to sign. It is total bullshit that you are not given these to review well in advance of surgery day. I mean, really, do you expect me to read all this? I've just put my glasses in the big plastic bag anyway. I think there should be a simple rule: all my clothes off, too late to sign releases. You want me to sign your form? Ask while I'm still wearing shoes.

There was a previous surgery where I was asked to sign documents as they were wheeling me down the hall to the operating room. Including an acknowledgement that the surgeon might have a financial interest in the manufacturer of the device he was about to implant. What kind of bullshit is that? Please don't get me wrong, I am grateful to the doctors and healthcare organizations for my care, and I want the surgeons operating on me to be the rock stars – the ones that are inventing the devices, but I do take issue with some of their business processes.

So, back on the table in the prep area, the anesthesiologists come in to place an epidural. This will be an important part of the pain management following the surgery.

There seems to be a moment of panic and they double check to make sure I've signed their paperwork before puncturing my back and inserting the line somewhere between the lower end of my should blades. Between the waiver I've just signed and their repeated questions about how and what I am feeling, I get the idea that this is a little risky and it is making me a bit nervous. And that's sort of how all of this rolls out: on one level (from the doctors' point of view) this is all completely routine. All of this stuff they do to you, they've done a thousand times. But there is always some risk, a fact that I'm acutely aware of after all of the detours and fire drills we experienced during chemo therapy. After the epidural, there is some waiting and then it is time to say goodbye to my wife.

Since receiving the initial go-ahead for surgery, I've had about 2 months to contemplate this moment. Unlike some previous procedures, Sabrina is not allowed to walk with me down the hallway to the O.R. Two months of meditation and prayer. Two months of running the scenarios in my head. Two months of unsatisfying research into what happens next.

They wheel me down the hall and into the O.R. At least I think it's the O.R. The nurses and technicians and others start to gather. They are immediately moving me around, positioning me. "I" am an object on a table. There is a mask or spacer or insert in my mouth. Some medicine is injected. Fade to black.

Now I am conscious again. I have time-traveled and a moment later arrived here six hours in to my future. Sabrina and my Dad are standing over me. I am shaking uncontrollably. "The surgery went great. You are OK." Fade to black again. I am awakening. Still shaking. It is like jumping hard into the water but in reverse, repeatedly. Sabrina and my Dad are still there.

Going in, there was some question about what the surgeon would do if he encountered the metastatic lesions previously identified in my liver. The plan was ablation and then moving on to the main event: removal of the primary tumor in the pancreas and a significant portion of my digestive system. Sabrina shares the good news: "They couldn't find anything left in the liver to take out." I want my money back. The rest of the surgery went by the book.

I am moved up to the floor. No extended stay in an ICU or step-down.

When I arrive in my room, I'm finally able to take stock. There are four IV placements with six lines into them. Plus the epidural line to my back. There are telemetry leads stuck all over my torso. An oxygen line under my nose. Compression sleeves on my lower legs. A blood pressure cuff on my arm and a pulse oximeter taped to my finger. There is a Foley catheter…well, you know where that one is. Someone measures the output every now and then. A massive bandage covers my middle abdomen. There is a clear bulb hanging from one end for drainage. Someone measures the output every now and then.

And the best part is a nasogastric (NG) tube running up my nose and down the back of my throat into my stomach. It is hooked up to a vacuum pump. Someone measures the output every now and then.

There is a young doctor, a member of the surgeon's team, who comes in to visit. He explains that my digestive system has been shocked by the surgery and that it will take a while for it to wake up and start working again with all of the components moving together in the right direction. I make a joke about a South Park episode (the one where they poop "backwards") which goes over the doctor's head. I suppose he does not have a lot of time for watching television, and I am drugged up enough that I feel the need to explain it to him. He humors me.

The torturous routine of my hospital stay begins. Every hour my finger is pricked and squeezed for a blood test to see if I am turning diabetic – this goes on around the clock for 2 or 3 days. Every four hours I am stuck in the arm for a blood draw – this continues around the clock for an entire week. Nurses are constantly coming in to change IV bags, administer medicine, correct an IV line occlusion, or clear a pump error. Between nurses and techs coming and going and IV pump alarms sounding, there is rarely a moment of peace in my room. Lights are turned on in the middle of the night and often people forget to turn them off on their way out. When the room is dark, the screen saver on the computer monitor in the room casts dancing shadows on the wall that startle me out of my haze. This hospital is a major regional trauma center, so helicopters are periodically flying in above me.

My first nurse on the first day is very young. Many of them are. Although this is a top-notch hospital, it is obvious as the days go on that they are in a perpetual scramble to cover shifts, especially overnight. But the nurse on the first day is a problem. I do not think she has handled a Whipple patient before and she seems very uncertain of herself and flat-out states that "no one told me you were coming." I need her to be confident. Or at least not let her doubt show and simply go get help when she needs it. She pushes a drug fast directly through my IV. My arm is burning. I've had enough. Get me a different nurse. Sabrina talks with the charge nurse and I do not see this person again. Although I never feel that my safety is a risk, I do feel that I need to remain aware and alert to what it going on with my care. That has been my approach through treatment up to surgery and I believe it is part of what has gotten us this far.

On the 2nd day I am moved to a private room. Also, the catheter is removed. Slowly, all of the things stuck on and in me will fall away over the course of the next week. These milestones will mark progress but there are a few wrinkles along the way.

A few hours after the catheter is removed, I am feeling the need to urinate. Strangely, I am not able to. The hours pass and this becomes a problem. Finally, the nurse gives me an ultimatum: pee or the catheter goes back in. Well, a watched pot never boils, right? So my bladder is full and the catheter goes back in. This occurs in the middle of the night. I am living a true 24 hour day, so the issues arise and I am on my body's schedule and the schedule dictated by the medical processes. The first catheter was placed when I was unconscious and being prepped for surgery. This time I am very much awake. Have you ever seen a Foley catheter placement kit?

Sabrina holds my hand during this event. A loved one's hand is good medicine. But like the pain medicine, it has its limits

The surgeon speculates that the epidural is impacting the muscles involved in emptying the bladder. Apparently, they see this situation sometimes…among the elderly. The pain management team insists it has nothing to do with the epidural. In any case, the catheter stays in until my second-to-last day at the hospital.

The next challenge is my NG tube. A portion of my stomach has been removed, so has the valve between the stomach and the intestine, along with the first portion of the intestine itself. What is left has been reattached. The connections are a source of potentially serious complications. This particular connection is also the source of a very common complication: delayed gastric emptying. Basically, the hole where fluid empties from the stomach swells closed and gastric juices back up in the stomach. They are pumped out through the NG tube. In my case, the tube keeps getting clogged.

There is an access line where they can flush it with saline. The nurse has to work the flushing syringe vigorously, like a toilet plunger, to clear the line. This keeps happening and I am miserable. At one point, I am taken for an x-ray to see if they need to reposition the tube. This involves a very surreal ride through the medical center, including passing through one of the lobbies and elevator rides with a random assortment of hospital staff and visitors. The clogging and flushing continue for a few days. If you saw the contents of the vacuum pump reservoir, you'd think my joke about the South Park episode was coming true.

The NG tube remains in place until day 4 or 5 when, after a day of clearing flow, it is removed. The nurse yanks it out surprisingly quickly. Covered in greenish bile and mucous, it looks and feels as if an eel has just been pulled from my nose.

The removal of the NG tube is a turning point. Up until now, I have been days without sleep, or food, or even liquid by mouth. The fatigue and all the drugs are taking their toll. Although I have been in the same room since day two, at different times of the day I do not recognize the room and think I have been moved. Also, the paint sometimes starts melting off the walls...upwards. One day, during rounds, the doctors come in and all smell strongly of alcohol. I think that they must have been celebrating something but that it is pretty early in the day for that. And I hope it is not impairing their judgment. It only occurs to me later that the odor of alcohol was actually just the smell of hand sanitizer.

Coincidentally, the physical therapist comes in shortly after the NG tube is removed and wants me to get out of bed. Um, no. "Doctor's orders" she says. Then send the doctor in and I'll tell him that I'm not getting out of bed. Come back later.

I've been getting out of bed since the first day. They really stay on you about getting up and moving, it is a key to recovery. Among other things, everyone is pre-occupied with bowel movements and by standing up and moving, gravity helps with that process.

On my first walk, I barely make it out of the room. Each day I can walk a little further, standing up a little straighter. They really stay on you about your posture. I am using a walker. The urine bag hangs from it, sloshing around with each stutter-step forward. Sabrina or a nurse handles the IV pump pole. The drainage bulb dangles from the side of my incision. My ass hangs out of my hospital gown.

The walls of the ward have inspirational messages written on them. I had noticed them after my staging laparoscopy surgery but had not read them or thought about why they're there. When it takes you 10 minutes to walk 20 feet, you have time to read what's on the walls. And now they make sense.

On my second-to-last day, the epidural comes out. A couple of hours later, I realize how much of a friend it has been. Even though I still have IV pain medicine, the entire area of my incision now burns. I'm told it is the myriad severed nerve endings doing what nerve endings do. Once the epidural is out, the drainage bulb comes out. Then the catheter, again.

I'm walking laps around the 16th floor now. They start me on a highly restricted diet. Toast and bananas or something along those lines.

And I am finally pooping. There is a free standing bed-side commode that I have been using. There is nothing like a half-dozen surgical residents walking in while you are taking care of business to give new meaning to the term "throne."

One final day at the hospital. The IV pain medicine has been removed and replaced with pills. Toward the end of the final day, all blood work is coming back clear, the pain is under control, I am mobile, the bowels are moving, the urine is flowing, and the kitchen is delivering 3 "meals" per day. Time to go home.

I met more caregivers than I will ever be able to remember. There were some truly exceptional ones that provided moments of light that helped me through this. Can you believe that people are so committed to working in a hospital that they train for years? I am grateful for all of them.

But looking back, I am surprised by the feelings of anger, and sadness, and fear that persist.

These days, between yoga class, my pancreatic cancer support group, doctor follow-ups, and labs, I am in a cancer facility of some sort at least once each week. All it takes is about 30 seconds sitting in an oncologist's waiting area, or really even passing through the cancer center lobby, and the anger and sadness are drained and replaced by gratitude. My compass is realigned...at least for a while.

The fear? Well, that's always there. The fear can be a headwind or a tailwind, it's up to you to choose. I read that in a magazine recently. It stuck with me.

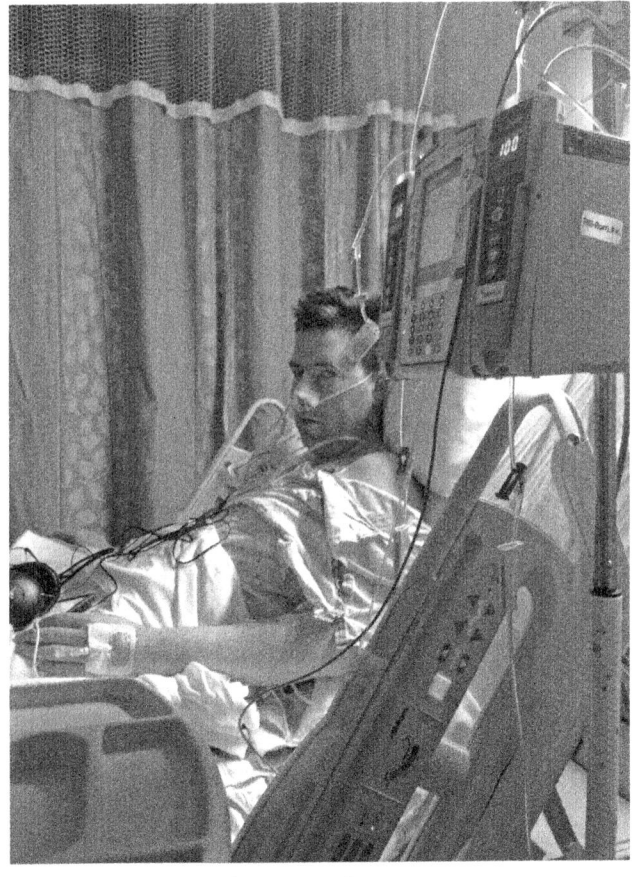

Surrender

The cancer is gone

Written Mar 6, 2014 2:17pm by Dave Robb

I am sitting at my computer for the first time in more than a month. They performed the Whipple on February 4th. I spent a week in the hospital and have been recuperating at home for the last several weeks. Most of that time has been spent in bed, but each week it gets a little better. The surgeon completely understated how difficult the recovery would be – or maybe that's just what all the doctors meant when they said it's a "big" surgery. The pain is mostly gone, but it is a struggle to eat and simple tasks, like taking a shower, can sometimes exhaust me and put me right back into bed. A nurse comes to the house every day and changes the packing/dressing on the open wound I have in my side as a result of an infection in my belly – but that seems to be the only lingering complication of the surgery.

My hospital stay included some of the most terrifying and painful moments of my life. To sum up, I've never felt so thoroughly defeated and exhausted, mentally and physically. Beaten into resignation and near delirium. Sabrina was right there next to me and helped me through – she's the most amazing person that I know. I'll probably give it all some thought and write about it some other time, but for now I am grateful that it is slowly fading in the rearview mirror. Classic cognitive dissonance because the surgery was a huge success.

We have achieved everything we worked for: the cancer is gone. This is miraculous.

After "completely mobilizing" my liver (which is a funny way of saying they pulled it out of my body while they were in there), the surgeons could not find any metastasis to address there, so I guess they just tucked it back in when they were finished with everything else. The pathology report showed complete success in the removal of the pancreas tumor. However, it also showed that, despite a year of chemo and radiation, etc., there were still active cancer cells in the tumor, so this surgery really was crucial to my long-term prospects.

In another month, we'll head to Houston again and circle together the oncologists and surgeon to decide next steps. This will most likely involve another 3 to 6 months of chemotherapy and then a plan for scanning intervals after that. They will probably recommend the FOLFIRINOX chemo regimen again. I've been giving some thought to this: last year that was scary, but I had nothing to lose; this time around, I can see the light at the end of the tunnel.

The snow continues to melt here and I am beginning to think about the Spring and our garden. Our sons are more than halfway finished with kindergarten. Rhys and Holden were preschoolers when this cancer journey began. Today we live in an entirely different world.

Many thanks to all of you for the cards, notes, dinner delivery, and overall support. So many people have helped our family – in ways large and small – and it has made all the difference in getting to this point.

Love,

Dave

Slow Spring, Slow Healing

Written Apr 7, 2014 4:28pm by Dave Robb

So my recovery is dragging out. The infection that presented itself about a week after I returned home from the Whipple has persisted and my wound is healing slowly. The infection made the wound very "angry" and trapped fluid forced it to open in another place. The surgeon attributes this to my body's healing capability being hindered by all the abuse it received during the chemo and radiation last year.

As a result, there was another surgery two weeks ago where they opened most of the length of the original incision and cleaned out the infection. I am now attached to a "wound vac." It works like this: the wound is packed with a sponge (or sponges) and a layer of adhesive plastic is applied to the skin making an air-tight seal. A suction cup and line are then attached to the dressing on one end and a vacuum pump on the other. The vacuum pump is not unlike my home infusion chemo pump for size and weight – it just operates in reverse. This approach creates a productive environment for healing and stimulates new tissue growth. Unfortunately, the new tissue grows around and into the packing sponge so some of the new tissue comes out along with the sponge during dressing changes – this happens three times a week. Despite my being loaded up with meds – it really hurts. Like scream-out-loud hurting. There is a very skilled and patient home health nurse that is helping me get through this. The wound is now closing very nicely and the dressing changes are getting much easier.

The ironic thing is that the culprit in the infection is just a common bacteria that lives on our skin.

Although this is taking a while and delaying getting back on the chemo that we anticipate, I keep reminding myself that in the past fifteen months that I've been battling with this, 40,000 people have died of pancreas cancer in the United States alone. Also, my most recent MRI and CT show no cancer and that everything is looking good with the reconfiguration that occurred with the Whipple. I have so much to be thankful for.

Two months ago, when the infection first presented itself, my incision ruptured and fluid flowed down my abdomen and legs: off to the emergency room! In case you've never been there, the Barnes ER is a place you don't want to be. Last time we were there was for Sabrina's bicycle accident a couple of years ago. The guy in the next bay – shackled in handcuffs - was under the guard of a police officer. This visit was comparatively quiet.

Holding a towel to my stomach to stop the fluid coming out of my gut, I stumbled through the metal detector and fumbled to empty my pockets of whatever was making it beep. Come on guys! I'm holding a bloody towel to my gut, maybe there could be an express line? I end up in the part of the ER where they take the gunshot wounds on a Saturday night. There is room for two patients in this space, which looks a lot like an oversized operating room. The other patient in the room is an old man – maybe around 80 years-old. It was a cold and icy morning and he had walked out to retrieve the newspaper from his driveway. He slipped and fell and had a stroke – right there in his driveway. Or maybe he had a stroke and then fell. In either case it's a bad one. He's just been wheeled back in from a scan of his brain. He can't speak and is urinating on himself and appears to be in pain. They are cutting away his clothing. There is a swirl of activity around this man. But some of the ER staff are just standing and observing – as if there will not be much that they can do.

Even the janitor pauses to watch for a moment as he passes by. I'm not sure why I remember that detail but I think it is this: there are many people in a hospital that you don't notice, but they notice you. Having made an effort to talk with some of them over the last year, I am struck by the discovery that many of these people, while not in a direct care role or in a lesser caregiving role, care a great deal about what is happening to people. For some people, it's just a job, but for a surprising number, they do their jobs thoughtfully and there is meaningful, healing energy generated by their devotion to their work.

The man's wife and daughter are there. The doctor explains that the scan reveals that this is a type of stroke that people usually don't recover from. The daughter is struggling to find a cellphone signal and is desperately trying to reach family so that they can come right away to the hospital. This is all like something right out of a TV medical drama – except that it is real. It is an intimate moment and I feel like an intruder – I really wish I wasn't there. I am reminded of a passage from The Great Gatsby where Nick Carraway remarks that he wants no more "privileged glimpses into the human heart." Nonetheless, my thoughts have been with this stranger and his family over the last couple of months.

We went to a wedding last weekend. There were ceremonies and dinners on both Friday and Saturday. Our sons were the ring bearers. They are both in love with the bride and were thrilled to be a part of things. I was so happy to see our friends get married. And it was great to be out with our family having a fun time. The bride's father beat cancer many years ago – and there he was, giving his daughter away at the alter and making a speech at the reception. More and more these days, I dare to let myself look further out onto the horizon.

Love,

Dave

I'm talking about tomorrow

Written Jun 18, 2014 8:08pm by Dave Robb

My sons woke up on a tear the other day about building a tree house. They put together a blueprint for a network of tree houses connected by zip lines including one that runs to a neighbor's house several blocks away. I picked up Holden from day camp that afternoon and he was still talking about it. I told him that I didn't think we had time right now to work on a tree house. He responded: "but Dad, I'm talking about TOMORROW."

We can talk about tomorrow now and even make plans. At the end of the summer we're going to the lake and we don't have to time it to coincide with a chemo cycle or a trip to Houston. My perception of time is shifting. The strange thing is that somewhere along the way I lost a year. In the type of back-of-the-envelope calculations that we all do to figure out time in mundane daily matters, my math keeps turning out wrong. Is it time to renew my license plates again? Didn't I just do this? Am I 45 years-old? Like Billy in *Slaughterhouse Five*, I'm a little unfixed in time. Or maybe I'm just stuck in 2013 or maybe 2012 BC (before cancer).

Last week they ran blood work, a big MRI, and a CT. Results were all clear. Not a single attribute in the blood work was out of tolerance.

A miracle.

I do take a pancreas enzyme replacement with meals in order to better digest what I eat, but my appetite is strong and my weight is steady and I'm trying to ease into some exercise.

I never spent a lot time asking "why me?" when I was diagnosed, but now I'm asking "why me?" in a different context. Why have I had such an exceptional response to treatment? Why do I have all this time that others don't? Will the cancer come back?

Scans again at the end of the summer. Meanwhile, what do I do now? What do I do tomorrow? And how do I make it count?

In all the time I was in treatment, I never went to one of the monthly pancreas cancer networking group meetings. With all these questions, I finally went last month. Now, it may be like Fight Club: first rule of Fight Club is there is no Fight Club. Or maybe it's like Las Vegas and what happens in group, stays in group. But I'm going to go out on a limb here.

The group is a mix of people who are actively undergoing treatment and those that have been through it and are currently living with no evidence of disease. And the majority of people in the room look to be around my age – that's scary.

In this day's group, one participant was convinced this disease will kill him and there is nothing that will alter that outcome. Another was convinced that nothing can harm her, she simply won't allow it. Two ends of the spectrum so far apart that they're really operating from flip sides of the same absolute platform. The rest of the group falls in the middle: we get up every day and do what we can with our lives and hope for the best. There was some serious humanity in that room. The group meets again next Thursday. I think I'll go.

Love,

Dave

Jumping into the pool

Written Aug 22, 2014 10:05am by Dave Robb

My regular lap swimming pool is closed this week so, Tuesday morning, Sabrina and I went to our town's outdoor pool to get some exercise. I have not actually been in that swimming pool since I was a kid.

As I swam my laps, the memories floated by. I remember how hot the concrete deck could be under my bare feet. I remember splashing in the kiddie pool when I was really little. I remember the shuffleboard court which was partially shaded by trees overhanging from the surrounding park. I remember the snack shack.

But the most salient memory that bubbled up was a visit to the pool one day when I was maybe 7 or 8 years-old. I was standing in the pool and there was another boy nearby who was perhaps 5 years-old - younger than my sons are now. The boy was lying on his stomach on the very corner of the apron of the pool. Back then, the apron was an aggregate concrete with unusually large river rock. It really hurt your feet to stand on it. Between the heat and the texture, I can only image what it felt like to lie on it.

The boy is crying and screaming and holding on to the pool deck as if he fears sliding off the side of the planet. He is in terror. But at the same time that he is clutching the deck, he is also inching slowly toward to pool. First a toe, then his entire foot. Dangling over the edge. He extends his foot and dips his toe into the water. Panic! He retreats and then tries again. This continues for a while.

I am ashamed to admit it but I remember feeling...disdain. Disdain in the way that we can sometimes fearfully regard someone who is struggling with something we take for granted. But I also felt badly for him. And I remember wondering, more than anything at the time, who could be so mean as to force this boy into the pool.

So these were the memories that swirled as I swam my laps.

Tuesday afternoon it was time for labs and scans again. An interval screening to look for any newly declared metastasis. This day's scan is an MRI with Eovist contrast. An hour lying in the tube. I've lost count of the number of times I've been scanned. For MRIs it's been at least 20.

Sometimes I'm Zen. Sometimes I just absorb the heat and vibration of the machine, listening to the blaring rhythmic beeping and buzzing, and staring up at the interior of the tube— my eyes struggling to focus in the small space.

Sometimes I cry. This is a problem because my arms are strapped down loosely at the elbows, one hand holds the rubber "panic" bulb, and the other hand has the contrast dye line wrapped around it. No way to reach up and wipe my face. Sometimes I cry to the cusp of sobbing, my chest heaving with stuttering breaths. This is a problem because it interferes with the technician's sequence of instructions to hold my breath and then breath and on and on as they slice their way through the scan.

This day I thought about the boy at the pool all those years ago. Lying in the tube, as a 45 year-old cancer survivor and father of young sons, the script flipped for me and I saw the situation in a completely different light: the little boy, despite his fear, was inching toward that pool. Despite the terror, he was trying to get in the water. Darn it, I was aiming for Zen. Instead I cried.

The labs are back. The radiologists have reviewed the MRI and the next day's CT. I've met with the oncologist and the surgeon. All clear! My good health – impossibly – continues.

In fact, my health is so good that this year I will be riding in the Pedal the Cause cancer research fundraiser. I hope you will consider making a donation to my ride.

Many thanks to those of you who have already contributed.

We'd also love to have you join our riding team. Not in Saint Louis? No problem, you can join the team as a virtual rider.

Love,

Dave

Holden at the pool

Scans, Yoga, and Season's Greetings

Written Dec 22, 2014 10:19am by Dave Robb

I have not written in a while. I think I have been waiting for an ending to the story that began two years ago, some sort of closure that I could write about.

Instead, I have been living in a state of perpetual denouement. There is no tidy end. No happily ever after. Although, we are living happily.

When you are in therapy, your life has a very specific rhythm that is timed to your chemo cycles and scans. Now that I am out of therapy and living nine months with no evidence of disease, there is a rhythm tied to periodic scans and lab work. Check-up weeks are stressful – I turn into a big bear and disengage a bit to keep myself calm and shelter my wife and sons from any fallout.

Recently, we had another round of scans. I go in for scans and labs and come back the following day for results and to talk with the oncologist. We could do it all in one day, but there are inevitable delays in lab work – particularly with the tumor marker number – and, now and then, the scans require closer study. So, the lesser of two evils is to just come back the next day for results. The lab results start to trickle through the on-line health portal. I get e-mails letting me know they're there. The mobile app is crap. I anxiously logon and wait while the download gets hung up. But the doctor only releases them through the portal when they're clear; so I know I'm OK, I just want to see it for myself.

The scans, however, are always a live conversation. This time, I am waiting in an exam room for an hour. I've waited longer for this doctor, but an hour (on top of a day) is a long time waiting for scans results. I am stretching and doing breathing exercises and listening to music. The anxiety eventually overtakes me. Why is the wait so long? Is the doctor trying to power through his routine cases so that he can drop the bad news and have the accompanying long conversation about next steps? Or am I the routine case today and it is someone down the hall where the bomb is dropping? This is the crazy thinking that happens.

The doctor strides into the exam room. He belts out the scan results before he has barely opened the door. Everything looks good. Come back again in the new year.

The time in between the scans is what you make it: I have returned to work full time, Sabrina lost her mother to the disease that had been slowly stealing her away for several years, my sons wrapped up their second season of soccer and started new activities, our washing machine broke – twice, our Pedal The Cause team raised a ton of money for cancer research (many thanks for your support), we celebrated my 46th birthday and our 14th wedding anniversary, Sabrina and I have been out on a few dates, I got a new car, our dog spent some time in the hospital – he is fine, we are moving soon to a new house, and now it is Christmas. We are looking forward and are excited about the future.

Recently, I have been going to yoga classes. The classes I attend are comprised of cancer survivors and those in active treatment. I like yoga. A lot of it has to do with your core. My middle is all chopped up, so it is good therapy. It is also very relaxing;

afterwards I feel like I've taken a couple of Klonapin – minus the somnolence and disorientation.

I swim a couple of times a week and bike when the weather permits. But the cancer is never too far away. Some days it feels like it is chasing me as I ride my bike. Some days it is thrashing around me as I swim my laps. I keep going and I beat it. But only for the day.

The locker room at our town's rec center can be a funny place. My sons think poop and farts and underwear and nakedness are all very funny. And ancient naked men shuffling around the locker room? Hysterically funny. When I go alone for lap swimming, I try to go mid-morning or mid-afternoon in order to have a better chance at my own lane in the lap pool. At that time of day, the typical man in the locker room – other than brigands like me who don't keep honest business hours – are old men. I like these old guys. And good heavens are they old. It is funny to hear them talk about their ills. There is gallows humor, determination, discussion of various ailments, resignation, and satisfaction at making it out of the house and getting in their exercise. There is talk of grandchildren and vacations to warm destinations. Can I indulge now in imaging my old age and everything that may come in between?

Time is passing. Our medical dream team is slowly fading into the horizon. The medical oncologist here is at cruising altitude in his career and he got a job offer back home in San Diego. The surgeon who was with us from the beginning was recruited away to be the head of surgery at an East Coast hospital.

So here we are at our current destination but still in transit, filled with gratitude and amazement at the journey.

Sabrina and I didn't send a Christmas card this year. Just didn't make the time to do it. Happy Holidays to each of you and best wishes for your health and peace in the New Year.

Love,

Dave

The Perpetual Present

Written Mar 14, 2015 10:24am by Dave Robb

This week I read a couple of essays by a man named Paul Kalanithi, a neurosurgeon at Stanford University.

Dr.Kalanithi wrote about facing his terminal lung cancer diagnosis and how it altered his perception of time: "the future, instead of the ladder toward the goals of life, flattens out in to a perpetual present. Money, status, all the vanities the preacher of Ecclesiastes described, hold so little interest..."

Speaking practically, it also created for him a dilemma in verb conjugation. In what tense do you live your life when facing metastatic cancer?

I can relate. These days, I am 26 months into my Stage 4 pancreatic cancer diagnosis. This is impossibly far into the tail of the statistical distribution. With no evidence of disease, my most recent conversations with my care team have been around stretching out the intervals between scans and lab work. The reassurance of clear scans is balanced against the anxiety created by the process and the prospect of facing adverse results. At some point, the close surveillance is more upsetting than helpful.

This carries a shift again in my perception of time, distance to the horizon, and verb conjugation. Is it true or accurate or helpful to say that I "had" cancer, or do I "have" it still? My doctors choose their words carefully - partly for my benefit and partly because they just don't know; my case is outside of the norms and the probabilities. As Paul Kalanithi wrote: "Getting too deep into statistics is like trying to quench a thirst with salty water. The angst of facing mortality has no remedy in probability."

I met recently with the urologic surgeon (there was some brief concern about my prostate) and he does not want to see me again until I'm 50. No pink sheet for the front desk to schedule a follow up on my way out the door. There was a time when deferring a follow-up for four years would have sounded absurd. Today, it makes me feel like a normal 46 year-old.

There are cancer survivors who are permanently transformed by their journey and cancer continues to occupy a prevalent space in their lives. There are others who try to forget all about it, to push it into the past; some of them avoid going to the doctor.

I struggle to find a balance. This journey permanently transformed our family. But we also crave "normal."

Part of the new normal is that, through friends of friends, or further degrees of separation, I am regularly in touch with others who are facing pancreatic cancer. A gentleman yesterday asked about the pain. Early on, I remember being very fearful of the physical pain. The conversation took me back to those portions of my journey. In hindsight, the physical pain was not a true enemy, but I remember when it seemed that way.

Today, at this particular moment, living in our perpetual present, I choose to say that I "had" cancer. My sons' baseball season starts soon and I just bought my first-ever baseball mitt.

Dr. Kalanithi? He died last week of lung cancer. He was 37 years-old.

Love,

Dave

Living Between the Scans

Throughout this journey, as I write about it, I often dash off a journal entry and set it aside. I come back to edit it later and find that I reconstrue what I originally wrote about. Sometimes I surprise myself. Sometimes I have to force myself. The facts don't change, but somehow the story does.

Looking back, it always changes for the better. In fact, many of the best moments of my life have occurred in the last two years. Unfortunately, just about all of the worst moments have occurred during the same period. That's where it helps to set it aside and come back to it.

When this all began, I was not the cancer survivor I needed to be. To be honest with myself, I was not the father and husband I wanted to be. That part is still a work in progress.

Nor did I have a true belief system. Values, ethics, morals – I had those, but they were not a part of a larger belief system. Today, living between the scans, I believe there are three powers at work in our lives.

The first is the power of chance. Some choose to call it luck. I prefer the word "chance." Whatever you call it, much of life is shaped by random events. There is random bad: "Mr. Robb, the typical survival for someone with your diagnosis is about six months." And there is random good: "Mr. Robb, your cancer is showing an exceptional response to therapy."

People really have trouble with this one. The idea that no matter what you do, a huge portion of life is a matter of chance is really hard to accept. I think it is the powerlessness of it that is so hard to stomach.

There are some who say that that there is no such thing as luck, that you must make your own. Nonsense. But that is where the next power comes in.

The second power is the power of choice. This is making the best decisions based on the best available information. It is choosing to work hard. It is choosing to work toward acceptance. It is choosing to be responsible for yourself and others. It is choosing to hold yourself accountable.

The final power is the power of faith. I believe that there are connections and energy all around us. This energy and connectedness are at once very local and intimate yet simultaneously vast and unknowable. There are different words for this. God is the best word I can think of to describe my understanding. This is also where the help comes from. There are numerous people, many unexpected, who provided help in ways that have changed the course of my life. How is it that our lives intersected?

My cancer journey has taught me that the power of choice and faith give one the tools to navigate the randomness and find meaning along the way. Operating from these beliefs, I've learned a lot:

1. Everyone is different, what works for me may not work for you.

2. Always get a second opinion, even if things are going well. Do this sooner rather than later.

3. Everyone in the world now falls into one of two categories: in the boat with you or not in the boat with you.

You will be surprised by some of the people you think should be in the boat but aren't. You'll be even more surprised by those you have to throw overboard. There will be some strangers in the boat – you'll be grateful to have them, they will be among the greatest blessings.

4. Let God be a part of it.

5. Cut yourself some slack.

6. Cut other people some slack.

7. Don't waste time with regrets or blaming yourself.

8. Let go of everything that does not matter. That's hard at first, but gets easier

9. It's your cancer, feel and talk about it however you want. Want to talk about fighting and use battle metaphors, go for it. Want to use a different lexicon, that's good, too.

10. People, including doctors, will say some really dumb stuff. Try to shrug it off. Most people have good intentions but just don't have the right words. Others are simply careless.

11. You are responsible for putting together and managing your care team. Nobody can do this job better than you.

12. Educate yourself on your cancer and treatment options.

13. Challenge your doctors. Ask them to explain things to you. Ask them to justify their opinions.

14. Speak up if you think something is wrong.

15. Speak up if you need help.

16. Take the pain medicine if you need it.

17. Take the chill pills if you need them.

18. Keep moving.

I offer this list with the hope that it might help someone else. It is also a reminder to myself. But wherever your journey may take you, please, keep moving.